NEO-CAPITALISM:
The One Where Everyone Wins!

By

Jim Green

DEDICATED TO:

Those who "get it": To digress slightly for illustration—the common denominator in all of our mass killings are assault rifles—so why are we dancing around the obvious solution—they must be banned! Those who get it know this—we also need to take other steps—but unless we ban assault rifles our gun crisis will continue, and raising the age to buy one is patently insane! Another "elephant in the room" we don't talk about—but which should have all of us terrorized: the millions of Americans—who in their delusion believe one can be a "Christian", and "vote Republican"—and then vote against *EVERYTHING* Christ stood for, and spoke out against! We should be terrorized because of the impact this ill-informed faction, which has Congress/America being in paralysis—See on Amazon: IT IS IMPOSSIBLE TO BE A CHRISTIAN, AND VOTE REPUBLICAN. Carrying on—the "get it" which is the purpose of this book is that going forward in the 21st Century: Work must become a legal right! Those who "get it" know this—we have no choice—and not to meet some liberal equality reason—as our ignorant use to sabotage our progress in America—we must do this to save capitalism...

Amen

ISBN-10: 1986247678

ISBN-13: 978-1986247672

PROLOGUE

The concept most wallowing in ignorance in our current capitalism is that: *WORK MUST BECOME A LEGAL RIGHT!*

We will get there eventually—but least understood is that: FULL EMPLOYMENT IS A PRO-MARKET CONCEPT, Amazon/Kindle. It is foolish in a robot-driven economy---not to embrace the legal right to employment!

The right to work and be a productive member of society is a human right, and must become a legal right—a given in primitive societies, the concept was lost in the Age of Industrialization—to the detriment of our civil order ever since….

The dilemma standing in the way of our evolution are two colliding forces: One, the archaic belief that the market can provide everybody with a job—our sole method of job creation since WW II, and to this day—a belief that PURE BS—and has not resulted in an unemployment [hereafter UE] rate below 3% since 1953!

[Another component in this archaic belief—that we never talk about—is a segment of the oligarchy, with deep seated feelings of inferiority [including Trump]—who still have one foot on the plantation—and feel regarding the American employee the same as racists feel regarding blacks, i.e., they assuage their feelings of inferiority with the crude saying "If you are not better than a black, who are you better than?"....i.e., used by some in the oligarchy re employees, in their need to make themselves feel superior!]....

But in our ignorance re market job creation, we have left millions jobless in its wake, turned our inner-cities into war zones with drug economies, and created an epidemic of gun violence!

As a result of this relic belief of the past we, to this day, stand on one foot and then the other—waiting on the market to solve our UE problems—with a mindless indifference when it is obvious that it doesn't work! Indeed, it is as if we had a brain-freeze in which we pretend this is working—when all of the data tells us it is a miserable failure!

To illustrate, and few Americans seem to know this—but at the time GM was pulling out of Flint we had on the books the "legal authorization" to restrict Flint's UE to 3%--permanently [Humphrey-Hawkins, 1978]—

But rather than enforcing this law—we treated the law as if it were written on TP—and instead, we stood on one foot and then the other—clinging to the belief that the market would fix--and let Flint rot into decay—as well as the rest of the Rust Belt—with the lingering resentment ushering in the Trump presidency—and incalculable damage to America!

Secondly, in our dilemma to fix UE--is an immovable force—the future —with one study showing that within 12 short years, 2030, robots [automation] will replace 800 million jobs by 2030!

And, which in truth, for those paying attention—does not come as a surprise——in every election since 1980, and with growing timber, the number one issue has been JOBS, JOBS, JOBS—because of the ever expanding use of automation!

Maybe we should call it "creeping automation"….and yet, the current consensus in Washington is still to stand on one foot and then the other waiting on the market to fix our UE crisis—i.e., a position that is *PATENTLY INSANE!*

Common sense alone tells us that when a person is not employed—the loss of their income to the economy, has an adverse impact on the economy—

Common Sense, folks—and when we think of one individual, it is, of course, miniscule—but when we throw in the 7 million the DOL officially reports are looking for work but can't find any—[because there isn't any!]...plus their true estimate—15 million---we are talking about a significant loss of income to the market!

The "big lie" is that the market can provide everybody with a job—*IT IS PURE BS!*

And our current capitalists never talk about this—indeed, their minds still have one foot on the plantation—and for many, American employees are seen as: A POOL OF SLAVES TO BE USED AND DISCARDED "at will", Amazon/Kindle—and they foolishly overlook at the loss of income to the economy as a result of their ignorance!

The black-hearted Republicans in Congress, to this day, hate the thought of the American employee having "rights"!

Indeed, since WW II the Koch brothers [a metaphor, and fact, for the 1%] have spent hundreds of millions buying governors, legislators, Congress—with the specific purpose of eliminating "rights" for the American employee, and in destroying the union movement—

In fact, every state now has "at will" employment laws [only Montana limits to probationary employees], and half of our states suffer from union busting legislation—as a result of selling our elections to the highest bidder!

To illustrate, at the close of WW II President Truman was faced with finding employment for millions of returning troops—and he advocated for THE FULL EMPLOYMENT BILL OF 1945.

When the Republicans in Congress [who were in majority] got their dirty hands on the Bill, however, it was reduced to suggestions—rather than a Bill of substance and became law as the EMPLOYMENT ACT OF 1946.

Ironically, Australia was faced with the same problem—and they did, in fact, take the position that anyone wanting to work, should be able to find a job—with the result that for most of the next 30 years their unemployment [hereafter UE] rate was 2%, or less—and the Australians stiil refer to this era as their "Golden Age".

And it would still exist, but was destroyed when the ill-wins of conservatism swept across the world and brought us Reagan and Thatcher—and now the Australian UE rate is rarely below 6%! And their sluggish economy is reflective of this poor thinking!

Truman did set in motion the concept of full employment, however, and laid the groundwork for the passage of Humphrey-Hawkins, in 1978—*THE MOST IMPORTANT LAW PASSED IN THE 20TH*

CENTURY—and more relevant every day in the 21st Century—as illustrated above! [more on this later].

To expand briefly on the importance of full employment to the health of the economy—a truism is that UE is a NO ONE WINS! The jobless lose, civility loses [Ferguson, etc.,], and the market loses, to wit:

THE LAW OF DIMINISHED INCOME TO THE MARKET RESULTING FROM UNEMPLOYMENT [hereafter D/UE LAW]

3% is the zero-sum threshold above which unemployment diminishes labor training and skills, under-utilizing capital resources, reducing the rate of productivity advance, increasing unit labor costs, reducing the general supply of goods and services--and the loss in income to the Market is compounded exponentially with each percentage point of increase in unemployment, above 3%.

Short Definition:

3% is the zero-sum threshold above which unemployment starts substantially undermining the Market--and the loss in income to the Market is compounded exponentially with each percentage point of increase in unemployment, above 3%.

I am a capitalist—support 100%, build a better widget, sell it for a million bucks, and retire in Florida—and to give a name to our Neo-Capitalism, I coined the term ECONOMIC INCLUSIVISM—and published a book for Amazon: ECONOMIC INCLUSIVISM: NEO-CAPITALISM/AN ANTHOLOGY—and created a web site: www.Inclusivism.org --which has been on the internet since 1996.

The irony in all of this is that we have a "conservative" concept [albeit it sounds wildly radical] entitled "universal basic income" [UBI] that each year applicable citizens would be given a fixed grant—tossed around is $10,000—to be infused back into, and to keep the market healthy…..[with the right to work vastly superior]—but nevertheless, used here to illustrate—full employment is a PRO-MARKET concept…. "get it?"….

A few closing comments in the Prologue—As Oscar Wilde averred "The only truly worthless opinion is an unbiased one" ….So bias, yes, but always in search of the truth….

Incidentally, I published my first book on my 78th birthday [I am currently 83]—and not that I write that fast, or well—the materials were all there for the better part of the past 30 years, give or take, gathering dust—it was just a matter of pulling them together in my style [some like, some don't….but always strive to communicate with the reader—i.e., I frequently add my book titles to FACEBOOK-and one of my favorites is IT IS IMPOSSIBLE TO BE A CHRISTIAN, AND VOTE REPUBLICAN—if you read my reviews on Amazon they are filled with hate messages—I didn't change any minds—but I did communicate with the reader…capish]—also, don't believe any book should be over 60 pages, plus/minus— i.e., can be read in the crapper--two hours, max--lol—but it seems best summed up by a very astute observer [wish I could recall their name to give credit]: Persons who write do so because they have no choice [it is a compulsion, an addiction..]—they become an "author", however, when people start reading what they have written….

Finally, a note to the reader—the papers and letters are not in sequence, and apologize for redundancy [please look for the nuggets…Thx--lol]—also, if you are a "typo-wonk"—are more concerned with sentence structure, etc., than content—you probably won't like my writing—and you will find a wayward capital letter, here and there, and appearing out of place and used for emphasis—or a missing page…Hey, I'm an Indie….I chalk most up to editorial license and tongue-in-cheek, self-effacing humor—so apologies, here—[I seriously support: Take what you do seriously, but never yourself….]….

Just look for content, please…..THX

CHAPTER ONE

President Obama:

It is impossible to reform our broken criminal justice system—absent our creating a viable job creation program in America.

And while it is generally believed that we do have a job creation program, in fact, we do not!

We have the BELIEF that "the market can provide anybody wanting a job, with a job"—but the data shows that only ONCE since WW II has this belief resulted in an unemployment rate below 3%--in 1953—leaving millions jobless in its wake-- and has resulted in:

60% minority unemployment in our inner-cities, with drug economies, and an epidemic of homicides [i.e., not fixing unemployment has turned our inner-cities into war zones, and created a breeding ground for our inexplicable incarceration rate].

Further this "belief" has been a stumbling block in finding a solution for our pervasive unemployment--In short, we have not been looking for a solution—because our policy makers believe we have one—and apparently few have looked at the data….

Also, ignored in the discussion is that unemployment is a "social" problem, with adverse, and oft severe social consequences—both for the individual, as well as the larger society [i.e., it is the responsibility of the larger society to solve]—

With tentacles integral to all of the social problems facing Americans, today—for instance, ending unemployment is integral to Criminal Justice Reform, and the repair of our crumbling infrastructure....

Further, in 1975 we spent $5 educating our youth, for every $1 we spent on prisons.....by the mid-1990's [with the American people having been terrorized by the Willie Horton ad—and on an hysterical prison building spree] our competing tax dollars tipped in favor of prisons—and at present we spend more on prisons, than on educating our youth.

The irony in all of this is that we have the "legal authorization", on the books to reduce our unemployment rate to 3%, tomorrow [15 USC § 3101—and deficit-neutral HR 1000, currently in Committee]—and also ignored in this context, is that President Obama had a weapon in addressing our economic meltdown in 2008, not available to FDR—and that is the $800 billion in Social Security Insurance claims percolating up through our economy—and in the absence of which--We would be buried in another Great Depression!

Turning the page—and given "automation", alone, is critical going forward in the 21st Century—and is a "win-win"—the American people win, and the market wins....

Ref: **FULL EMPLOYMENT IS A PRO-MARKET CONCEPT, Amazon**

Jim Green, Democrat opponent to Lamar Smith, 2000

CHAPTER TWO

President Obama/Council of Economic Advisers:

A puzzlement for years—what is it about Washington that will not let it accept that UNEMPLOYMENT [hereafter UE] is what caused Flint [the Rust Belt] to fall into decay?

Had it been a pandemic that ravaged Flint, the reason would have absolute clarity—and we would have marshaled every resource at hand to eradicate the cause as rapidly as possible—but with Flint, Washington stood idly by and let the city implode....WHY?

In fact, Flint went from a robust city of 80,000, with little crime in 1978, to a slum with a population of 50,000 by 1992--the highest crime rate in America, and an epidemic of gun violence!

What is all the more puzzling about this phenomenon, is that it is hardly off the political radar, with almost 1 in 2 Americans [43%] citing JOBS as the #1 issue in the 2016 election—

And, Governor Kasich in a speech, today, cited Job Creation as the SINGULAR goal of politicians—for example, at the time GM inexplicably abandoned Flint, we had the legal authority, on the books, to limit Flint's UE to 3%--IMMEDIATELY [15 USC § 3101]—i.e., at no time should the UE rate in Flint exceed 3% [to this day]--but our politicians were impotent [or indifferent] in enforcing this LAW…..WHY?

Further, twice since WW II America has stepped up to the plate to address UE head on—with the [FULL] EMPLOYMENT ACT OF 1946, and the HUMPHREY-HAWKINS FULL EMPLOYMENT ACT, in 1978 [above]—but rather than being implemented—Americans were duped by the oligarchy [and our elections awash in cash, and magical thinking] into believing "the market can provide everybody wanting a job, with a job"—which the data to this day shows to be pure BS!

In short, UE is a NO ONE WINS—the jobless lose, civility loses, and the MARKET LOSES—people do not buy what we manufacture when they are jobless….and the Market has an exponential loss in profit with each UE point increase above 3% [the D/UE LAW]…..

The over-arching point, here, is that given the damage [with Flint as the proof] UE should be seen as no different than a pandemic—and there is a moral lapse by our failure to eradicate UE, the same as we would a pandemic….

Ref: Deficit-neutral HR 1000 [in Committee], THE NEIGHBOR-TO-NEIGHBOR JOB CREATION ACT, and FULL EMPLOYMENT IS A PRO-MARKET CONCEPT, Amazon/Kindle

Jim Green, Democrat opponent to Lamar Smith, Congress, 2000

Thank you for contacting the White House!

CHAPTER THREE

President Obama/Council of Economic Advisers:

Two-thirds of the world's 7 billion population live in market-driven economies—1.2 billion are in the OECD, with China and India, alone, adding an additional 2.6 billion, and anyone who doesn't think China is a market economy, hasn't shopped at Wal-Mart….

The over-arching point, here, is the unwritten, but nevertheless pervasive/pernicious belief in our market-driven economies is that "the market can provide anybody wanting a job, with a job"….it is pernicious because it causes the "rank and file" to oppose climate change—in their belief that this is their *ONLY* means to get a Job! And, when, in fact, it is *BS, NOT* supported by the data or empirical evidence….

With the result that our record in job creation is deplorable—i.e., this methodology is woefully inadequate, as we inch along, and 5 years after the declared end of the Great Recession—we still have almost 10 million jobless Americans….

The question *NOT* being asked in Washington is: How do we address our pernicious unemployment in America—when the market cannot create enough jobs?

Had we put a lawnmower engine in the Saturn V rocket, on our Apollo 11 trip to the moon—we would never have gotten there…a perfect metaphor for our current method of job creation in America—which leaves millions jobless for years—and skewed against minorities…..

The fact is, *ONLY ONCE* in the past 65 years—under our "market only job creation" model—has our unemployment rate dropped below "3%"—in 1953—and in spite of the "legal authorization" in the U.S., since 1978, to limit our unemployment to 3% [15 USC § 3101].

In short, at *NO* time since 1978, and to this day, should our unemployment rate in America exceed 3% [HR 1000]---

And the irony is that unemployment is a "NO ONE WINS" proposition—both the jobless lose, and the market loses, to wit:

> 3% is the zero-sum threshold above which unemployment starts substantially undermining the Market--and the loss in income to the Market is compounded exponentially with each percentage point of increase in unemployment, above 3%.
>
> **FULL EMPLOYMENT IS A PRO-MARKET CONCEPT [Amazon]**

Jim Green, Democrat opponent to Lamar Smith, Congress, 2000

CHAPTER FOUR

President Obama/Council of Economic Advisers:

A German-national advised—in response to a question perplexing me for years—"Why on earth did the German people, with their rich cultural history, fall under the spell of a monster like Hitler"? And without a moments hesitation he said "Because he put them to work".

There is a message in there of vital importance: The value humans place on being a productive member of society—the value we place on "work"—even raising the question if it should become a Human Right?

And while giving lip service to the plight of the unemployed--our market economies, the OECD, which includes the U.S., all suffer from high unemployment—and none address unemployment as a "social" problem—with serious social consequences--WE, as a society have the RESPONSIBILITY to address—Rather they leave the creation of employment up to the whims of the market--And if the market fails, the unemployed are out of luck!

Which raises the question: The market suffers when people are unemployed—and the unemployed suffer when they are not working—so WHY on earth do our market-driven economies continue down such an unrewarding--a lose-lose path—where the market loses, and the unemployed lose?

The late Peter Drucker advocated for CEO salaries being limited to 20 times that of the lowest paid employee [the Swiss recently had on the ballot 12 times]—but it is argued that a brain-drain would occur if we didn't leave this to the market to set CEO salaries—

And whether or not this is true—WHY on earth do we persist in the anachronistic BELIEF that the market can provide anybody wanting a job, with a job [untrue since the mid-1970's]--particularly, and given automation, alone--an expanding and contracting public workforce is an INDISPENSABLE component to the EFFECTIVE functioning of a modern market economy?

Indeed, in the U.S. we have the "legal authority" on the books [15 USC § 3101], to limit our unemployment to 3%--in short, at no time should our unemployment exceed 3%--So why does Washington avoid this legal authority as if it were the plague—such as indifference to deficit—neutral solutions, i.e., HR 870, or via Social Insurance in The Neighbor-To-Neighbor Job Creation Act?

Please see: WHY WE CAN'T FIX UNEMPLOYMENT, Amazon

Highest regards,

Jim Green, Democrat opponent to Lamar Smith, Congress, 2000

CHAPTER FIVE

President Obama/Council of Economic Advisers:

Capitalism is ideal in producing and selling corn flakes and cars—It doesn't work in solving "social problems" such as unemployment and our healthcare....

And when we have tried "privatization" to solve our social problems—it has been a disaster:

Essential programs have been cut—such as the elimination of text books from the Job Corps education program—to increase profits, and cronyism has run rampant—

And in our "for profit" healthcare system, billions of dollars are siphoned away from the premiums we send in—and do not go to the healthcare of ANYONE—but rather is used to pay for lobbyists, to make the CEO's filthy rich—and spent on propaganda ads to keep it that way!

Further, it attracts a few who see healthcare as a means to get rich, rather than cure the ill....

The truth is, we currently have a blended system—and they are, in fact, indispensable to each other:

Were it not for Social Security Insurance moneys percolating up through our economy in 2008—we would not be talking about having narrowly averted another Great Depression—We would be buried in one!

Social Insurance is a vital ingredient in building a vibrant and decent society—And, invent a better widget, sell the company for a million bucks, and retire in South Florida [capitalism]—is as well a vital ingredient in building a vibrant and decent society.

So why do we have this war of words pitting the two against each other—rather than educating the American people regarding the indispensable symbiotic relationship they have to each other?

Were it not for the $2 trillion + Washington infuses into the economy annually—capitalism would fold in a NY Second!

And yet, most Republicans ask God in their prayers at night to be protected from becoming communists, or socialists, or even worse "liberals"—i.e., ignorant of what the terms mean…..

And this war of words disguises that the Republican Party, today, is not the Pro-Market party they boast—but rather their policies are, in fact, Anti-Market—destructive to capitalism!

Pandering to the GREED of their wealthiest contributors—the Republican One and Only program—is NOT a Pro-Market concept!

Another misnomer in the war of words, is right-wing invented "entitlement"—a word that should be banned from honest discussion—do we refer to our auto insurance as an "entitlement"?

And when Social Security Insurance brings in more that it pays out, i.e., is deficit-neutral--how is that an "entitlement", and why is it portrayed in our graphs as a "government expense"—or even included in these graphs? If a corporation reported a massive loss on a product they in fact made money—they would be charged with fraud in a New York Minute!

The list goes on—please see: OUR GREED AND IGNORANCE, on Amazon/Kindle

Jim Green, Democrat congressional opponent to Lamar Smith, 2000

CHAPTER SIX

President Obama/Council of Economic Advisers:

Our current method of Job Creation in America is a miserable failure—our proof is the fact that the number one issue in the 2016 election is JOBS—and we have had excessively high unemployment [hereafter UE] 70% of the time since 1980—[double that in prior years] with automation, alone, accelerating our UE the further we advance into the 21st Century.....

In truth, the world has changed and our UE crisis, with 20 million jobless Americans, is mired in the 18th Century as a result of Job Creation policies which have one foot on the plantation---in a 21st Century market economy--

Since WW II the oligarchy has spent tens of millions [buying elections/politicians] to look the other way, and turn their back on the will of the American people—i.e., and let the oligarchy write our Job Creation policy in America—it is based on the propaganda/lie that "the market can provide anybody wanting a job, with a job"—which the data shows to be Pure BS—

That is, only ONCE since WW II has this method of Job Creation resulted in a UE rate below 3%--in 1953—leaving millions jobless in its wake, and has resulted in 60% minority UE in our inner-cities, drug economies, and an epidemic of gun violence!

We need look no further than Flint to understand the destructive effects of unemployment--and WE are a "can do" nation—but when it comes to our Job Creation in America, our policies could be compared to our scientists putting a lawnmower engine in the Saturn 5 Rocket to the Moon…..

And the over-arching question, today, is: When our method of job creation doesn't work….why on God's earth do we continue down this path? And, particularly given the pervasive damage caused by UE--This criticism is not anti-capitalism—it is a statement of fact!

And ignored in all of this is that "We have far more work that needs to be done in America, than we have persons to fill these jobs", and "86% of Americans believe that anybody wanting to work should be able to find a job"…..UE is a NO ONE WINS: The jobless lose, civility loses [Ferguson, etc.,]…..

And, the Market loses!

INDISPENSABLE to the EFFECTIVE functioning of our market economy going forward in the 21st Century is: HR 1000 [in Committee], and/or THE NEIGHBOR-TO-NEIGHBOR JOB CREATION ACT, Amazon/Kindle—or like Job Creation….

Jim Green, Democrat opponent to Lamar Smith, 2000

CHAPTER SEVEN

President Obama/Council of Economic Advisers:

"The truth is poetry, problem is—most people hate poetry" Mark Twain

What if you knew something that would eradicate terrorism...but because of tradition, resistance to change, etc., your information is not readily understood....but at the risk of being stereotyped by the GE ad, and for the sake of discussion—here goes:

First, it needs to be understood that the most dangerous belief afoot in America today, is "the market can provide anybody wanting a job, with a job"—and while every Republican in Congress believes it to be true—it is dangerous, because it is PURE BS......

Indeed, so prevalent is this belief that it has dominated our Job Creation since WW II—and in spite of the fact that this has resulted in an unemployment [hereafter UE] rate below 3% only ONCE since WW II—in 1953—leaving millions jobless in its wake since, and has resulted in 60% minority UE in our inner-cities, drug economies, and an epidemic of gun violence —

Also, with the proliferation of automation, alone, in the mid-1970's, and subsequent loss of employment, we have had excessive UE 70% of the time in the U.S., since 1980—

Further, as a result of the paradigm shift in the 1970's, UE is accelerating the further we advance into the 21st Century....i.e., with 10% UE now common in the Eurozone--25% in Greece and Spain....and UE was a major factor in Arab Spring....

And here is where common sense comes in.....we need look no further than Flint, to understand the devastating results of UE, and statistics show that with each point of increase in the UE rate, 40,000 die in ancillary damage!

And yet, in spite of the damage, we have yet to identify UE as a "social" problem, ever bit as damaging as a pandemic—i.e., WE, as the larger society, have a solemn responsibility to address...but which we ignore with the rationalization that "No sweat, the market has this covered"....and Flint is the result.....

Finally, in this dynamic, the right to work and be a productive member of society was a given in primitive societies—but lost in the Age of Industrialization--and the indifference by the larger society to the importance of employment [inclusion], has become a breeding ground for terrorism.....

Ref: HR 1000 [in Committee], ECONOMIC INCLUSIVISM, and FULL EMPLOYENT IS A PRO-MARKET CONCEPT, Amazon/Kindle

Jim Green, Democrat opponent to Lamar Smith, 2000

Thank you for contacting the White House!

CHAPTER EIGHT

To The Honorable President Obama:

HR 1000 [In Committee] IS INDISPENSABLE IN OUR WINNING THE WAR AGAINST TERRORISM

This letter is to urge you to award the Presidential Medal of Freedom to U.S. Representative John Conyers, from Michigan.

Not only is he the longest-serving member of Congress—he has tirelessly worked for the Full Employment of Americans [HR 1000, in Committee], and in addressing inequity in America—a Renaissance Man in our 21st Century economy, who was present in Selma, on Freedom Day, October 7, 1963.

Further, Representative Conyers has made "an especially meritorious contribution to the security or national interests of the United States, world peace, cultural or other significant public or private endeavors" [the purpose for this award].

Few Americans are more deserving.

Finally, his appointment will call attention to the most important legislation in the 20th Century in our War On Terrorism, and indispensable to the effective functioning of our 21st Century market economy—pro-market Humphrey-Hawkins Full Employment Act, signed into law by President Carter [15 USC § 3101]. We have had excessive unemployment 70% of the time since 1980 as a result of automation/globalization, alone, and the implementation of this law [integral to HR 1000] will address the number one issue in the 2016 election: Jobs in our 21st Century market economy.

Ref: FULL EMPLOYMENT IS A PRO-MARKET CONCEPT, Amazon/Kindle

With highest regards,

Jim Green, Democrat candidate for Congress, District 21, TX, 2000

Thank you for contacting the White House!

CHAPTER NINE

President Obama/Council of Economic Advisers:

Every credible economist agrees that "High and persistent unemployment has pervaded almost every OECD country since the mid-1970's"....and almost 1 in 2 Americans [43%] cite Job Creation as the Number One issue in the 2016 election....

And yet, addressing the devastating results of unemployment [hereafter UE], as a stand-alone problem, to be solved the same as we would look upon a pandemic, is not in any of the debates, and while all of our candidates say they will create JOBS, our current solution to UE is analogous to not putting gas in our car, and then puzzling over why it doesnl't run.....and we need look no further than Flint, to understand the devastating results of UE.....

For instance, since WW II, the American people have been sold a Bill of Goods that "the market can provide anybody wanting a job, with a job"—which the data shows to be pure BS....and only ONCE since WW II has this Job Creation methodology resulted in a UE rate below 3%--in 1953—leaving millions jobless in its wake—and resulting in our inner-cities becoming war zones, with an epidemic of gun violence.....

And while all of the candidates talk about how they will create jobs, the REAL issue--the adverse consequences of unemployment —both to the jobless and the market…never gets discussed…..i.e., UE is a NO ONE WINS…the jobless lose, civility loses [Ferguson, etc.], and the market loses, to wit:

THE LAW OF DIMINISHED INCOME TO THE MARKET FROM UNEMPLOYMENT [hereafter D/UE LAW]

> 3% is the zero-sum threshold above which unemployment triggers inflation by diminishing labor training and skills, under-utilizing capital resources, reducing the rate of productivity advance, increasing unit labor costs, reducing the general supply of goods and services--and the loss in income to the Market is compounded exponentially with each percentage point of increase in unemployment, above 3%.

Finally, it would be ideal if the market could provide all of the jobs we need—but pretending that the market can provide a solution it is INCAPABLE of providing is analogous to our putting a lawnmower engine in the Saturn V rocket to the Moon…..

Ref: HR 1000 [in Committee]; THE NEIGHBOR-TO-NEIGHBOR JOB CREATION ACT, and FULL EMPLOYMENT IS A PRO-MARKET CONCEPT, Amazon, Kindle

Jim Green, Democrat opponent to Lamar Smith, Congress, 2000

CC: Donald Trump

CHAPTER TEN

President Obama/Council of Economic Advisers:

Our network of market-driven economies [the OECD, including the U.S]—currently have a pernicious job creation modality—with resulting high and pervasive unemployment since the mid-1970's—and on a collision course with the future—i.e., given "automation", alone, fewer and fewer jobs are being created with each passing year, as we advance into the 21st Century….

This job creation modality is based on the erroneous propaganda/belief that "the market can provide anybody wanting a job, with a job"—and yet, only ONCE since WW II has this modality resulted in an unemployment rate below 3%--in 1953—leaving millions jobless in its wake, and has resulted in our inner-cities turning into war zones--with 60% minority unemployment, drug economies, and an epidemic of homicides.

The irony in this disaster, however, is that the U.S. correctly anticipated this result in 1978—and provided the American people with a solution, i.e., the "legal authorization" [15 USC § 3101] to limit our unemployment henceforth to "3%", and as we advance into the 21st Century—

With a ton of cash poured into our political system, and a mind-set with both feet planted on the plantation—-special interests sabotaged this law to prevent its implementation—to the detriment of Americans, and America [ISIS is the least of our worries in America, when we have the Republican party]!

Unemployment is a "social" problem, with adverse social consequences….it is solely the province of the larger society to solve—and leaving the solution to anything as erratic as the market—as we do now—is patently absurd!

The bottom line is that unemployment is a NO ONE WINS….the jobless lose, civility loses, and the market loses, to wit:

THE LAW OF DIMINISHED INCOME TO THE MARKET FROM UNEMPLOYMENT [hereafter D/UE LAW]

> 3% is the zero-sum threshold above which unemployment triggers inflation by diminishing labor training and skills, under-utilizing capital resources, reducing the rate of productivity advance, increasing unit labor costs, reducing the general supply of goods and services--and the loss in income to the Market is compounded exponentially with each percentage point of increase in unemployment, above 3%.

Ref: HR 1000 [in Committee], and FULL EMPLOYMENT IS A PRO-MARKET SOLUTION, Amazon

Jim Green, Democrat opponent to Lamar Smith, 2000

Thank You!
Thank you for contacting the White House

CHAPTER ELEVEN

Folks, if you have gotten this far then you are aware that if we don't win the election, we don't get to make the changes we need to make to adapt to a changing world….and our current system is like a banker leaving the vault open to anyone coming into the bank…..for instance, if Walmart handed us a receipt for our purchases with the words "trust us"—we would be outraged, and yet that is a conummate metaphor for our current electronic voting…but, here, it is our democracy that is at stake…in any case, I created the following as a proposed solution…..

THE FAIL-SAFE ELECTRONIC VOTING ACT

EVERY electronic voting machine (hereafter EVM), must be inexpensive, identical throughout the U.S. in a 1/150 ratio, and *must count and produce a hard-copy of the recorded votes.* In addition, an extra copy of their recorded votes would be produced (not necessarily a hard-copy), marked "Voter's Copy", and containing "NOTICE: Do Not Destroy Until Every Election On Your Ballot Is Certified".

2) *After confirming that their votes are recorded correctly*, the voter would then insert the hard-copy ballot into a software-free (count only) optical scanner (hereafter OS), for a second count. The hard-copy ballot would be retained by election officials in the event a candidate asks for a recount (<u>*not possible under the current system, and which undermines the legality of*</u>

each such election). **The EVM and the OS must be manufactured by different companies (which is universally true today).**

3) **Election officials assigned to oversee the EVM, would be prevented by law from overseeing the OS, and vice-versa, and stiff criminal penalties would be imposed for violations.**

4) **Further, every EVM would be programmed with raw data re the total registration rolls, by party, and norms for their voting history, etc.,----as an "alert" to a possible irregularity, such as an "under-vote"—or "vote-flipping" etc., and <u>standards</u> established to suspend certification where there is an "improbable result", at least temporarily, of a particular election until the discrepancy is cleared up. (This is what computers do best, and it would be very easy to create such a program).**

5) **At the end of the election day, tallies would be taken from the EVM and the OS, for each election.** *If the tallies didn't balance for any given election, or if there is an "alert", that election cannot be certified until the "error" is corrected.* **If the candidates agree (the victory is certain), minor discrepancies in the count could be disregarded. While probably rare, the Voter, or a random sample of Voters, would be required by law to return their Copy of the recorded votes to the election office to clear up any "error", or where an "alert" signals the need for same.**

6) Further, every state provides for a recount when the total vote falls below a certain percent of difference between the candidates, impossible to conduct with the current EVM. And thus Congress must mandate the following regarding presidential candidates: A RUN-OFF election is mandated and triggered in those states where the percent of total vote is less than .025% of difference between the two candidates; said election to be held on the second Saturday following the election, on PAPER BALLOTS ONLY/RED OR BLUE—with the voter chosing the color to vote on [for an easy recount], and contain ONLY the names of the relevant candidates, for instance: "Barack Obama, Democrat" and "John McCain, Republican"—with oversight in counting by a representative(s) of each party—said procedure providing more than adequate time to meet the Electoral College mandate [Ideally, all of this could be eliminated if we did away with the Electoral College, but until then....]. NOTE: Had this been the law in 2000, Al Gore would be our president, and America would have been spared the economic, etc., disaster that followed!

7) Finally, absent the above safeguards, and until these safeguards are in place--Congress must mandate that PAPER BALLOTS, ONLY, can be used in our presidential elections. This is not a "partisan" issue, it is a "pro-democracy" issue. Most importantly, this will return the responsibility for our elections, and our vote counting, back into the hands of the individual voter, where it belongs, and out of the hands of "corporate control"---*it is after all "our democracy", itself, that is at risk if we don't take these steps---and in that regard, is*

there any time or cost differential that is too great?

Jim Green, Democrat candidate for Congress, 2000

CHAPTER TWELVE

President Obama/Council of Economic Advisers:

THE HISTORY OF HUMPHREY-HAWKINS

The historic March On Washington, and Dr. King's "I had a dream" speech, in 1963, was a march for JOBS.

At that time, and to this day, our job creation in America has been based on the premise that "the market can provide anybody wanting a job, with a job—

And yet, only ONCE since WW II has this method of job creation resulted in an unemployment rate below 3%--in 1953—leaving millions jobless in its wake.

Following Dr. Kings death in 1968, civil rights leaders, including Jesse Jackson, annually marched on Dr. King's birthday for legislation that would address our pervasive unemployment in America.

Their demand was not without legal foundation. In 1946, President Truman signed into law the [FULL] EMPLOYMENT ACT OF 1946, to provide employment for our troops returning from WW II.

The 1%, however, balked at American employees having rights—particularly a right to employment [the model which exists to this day]—and the law was never implemented.

Ironically, Australia enacted a law similar to President Truman's Employment Act—and for the same reason—and for the next 30 years [and until the ill-winds of neo-liberalism in the mid-1970's] Australia's employment model was based on the premise that "anybody wanting to work should be able to find a job"—with 2% or less unemployment common. Australians still refer to this as their "Golden Age".

As a result of the demand by civil rights leaders for legislation, however, in 1978 President Carter signed into law—what is commonly known as the Humphrey-Hawkins Full Employment Act [15 USC § 3101].

The law provides the "legal authorization" for the creation of a "reservoir of public employees" anytime our unemployment in America exceeds "3%". That is, and to this day—at no time should our unemployment rate in America exceed 3%.

The money in politics, however, has prevented this law from being implemented!

Notwithstanding, a lone Congressman, Conyers [and a growing number of co-sponsors] has diligently worked to implement Humphrey-Hawkins [currently, deficit-neutral HR 1000, in Committee].

And, singularly, unemployment is the most pernicious problem facing America, today....

Ref: FULL EMPLOYMENT IS A PRO-MARKET CONCEPT, Amazon

Jim Green, Democrat opponent to Lamar Smith, 2000

Thank You!

Thank you for contacting the White House.

CHAPTER THIRTEEN

THE HISTORY OF HOW WE GOT WHERE WE ARE
[WW II to Present]

Following WW II, President Truman signed into law the [FULL] EMPLOYMENT ACT of 1946, to provide employment for our returning troops.

Ironically, half-way around the world, Australia codified into their law an almost identical Bill, and for the same reason—

Difference is—Australia actually put their law into effect, and over the next 30 years it was intrinsic to employment policy in Australia that "anybody wanting to work should be able to find a job"—and save for a brief recession in 1961/62 their unemployment was 2%, or less. This period is still referred to as their "Golden Age", in Australia.

Unforeseen by either country, however, in the mid-1970's the world economy underwent a major paradigm shift as a result of the colliding forces of automation, globalization, technology, etc., reaching a critical mass—in brief, an adjustment towards modernity—From a perverse perspective, we became victims of our success....

The instability caused by this transition, however, resulted in a malaise, and ushered in the ill-winds of greed-driven neo-liberalism with its indifference to unemployment, and the likes of Thatcher and Reagan—and the menace of this greed-driven agenda was exploded by Bush II, resulting in obscene disparities in wealth that persists, and is the cause of much friction between right and left, to this day.

It also ushered in high and pervasive unemployment throughout our market-driven economies, the OECD—with 6% unemployment in Australia now the norm, and double-digit unemployment common throughout the Eurozone, to this day.

As a result of the "malaise", however, the U.S. took an aggressive, pro-active role in addressing the, above, economic shift—and in 1978 President Carter signed into law one of the most important laws in the 20th Century--an expansion of President Truman's full employment, i.e., Pro-Market 15 USC § 3101--which provides a "_legal authorization_" to create a "reservoir of public employees" [_indispensable to the effective functioning of a 21st Century market economy_]--at any time our unemployment in America exceeds "3%"—

But in spite of 3% unemployment being the threshold point above which unemployment starts substantially undermining the Market—this _legal authorization_ has never been implemented--

And in spite of deficit-neutral HR 1000, or The Neighbor-To-Neighbor Job Creation Act—A federally mandated Social Insurance, owned by our employed, to provide a fund to hire/train our unemployed—[more on the critical need to apply this job creation methodology in a 21st Century market economy, ahead]....

Ref: **FULL EMPLOYMENT IS A PRO-MARKET CONCEPT**, Amazon/Kindle

Jim Green, Democrat opponent to Lamar Smith, Congress, 2000

CHAPTER FOURTEEN

THE HISTORY OF HOW WE GOT WHERE WE ARE

[Mid-1970's to Present]

In the mid-1970's, the colliding forces of automation, technology, globalization, etc., reached a critical mass—resulting in a Market no longer capable of producing the jobs necessary to its viability, and causing ubiquitous unemployment in all of the OECD countries—and leaving their leaders conflicted, ever since, regarding the displaced employee. Eurozone unemployment is still in double digits, and Greece and Spain both in excess of 20%, plus. High unemployment was also a major factor in Arab Spring.

In the U.S., we took a pro-active role in addressing this economic shift—and in 1978 President Carter signed into law 15 USC § 3101--which "authorizes" the creation of a "reservoir of public employment" at any time our unemployment in America exceeds "3%".

In 1979, however, and in a panic over Humphrey-Hawkins—our ultra-conservative foundations, and desperate to promote the Supply-Side fraud, embraced a flawed paper by an obscure MIT student, David L. Birch "The Job Generation Process"; and [with lots of cash] gave his paper biblical importance, and every president since has cited his finding as gospel.

Birch's paper concluded that "small businesses" were the greatest generator of new jobs—problem is, for the purposes of policy-making—it is BS. In a study at Harvard University in 2010, "The Myth of Small Business Job Creation" The research shows "no systematic relationship between firm size and growth." And that small businesses can actually detract from job growth.

In spite of this, however, Washington struggles, still, to make this antiquated notion, work--that it is only the market that can create jobs—and the result has been a disaster, politically as well as otherwise!

It would be impossible to still have 7.8% unemployment—if we were on the right path—and among other problems with this concept--if the market fails, the unemployed are out of luck.

Further, unemployment is a "social" problem we are seeking to address with a highly unstable, incompatible entity: The Market

What apparently isn't clear going forward is that an expanding and contracting public workforce is an *indispensable* component to the *effective* functioning of a modern market economy—

The market thrives when we have a robust, employed, consuming workforce—and overlooked is that HR 1000 [currently in Committee], and the proposed "Neighbor-To-Neighbor Job Creation Act" www.Inclusivism.org [both authorized under Humphrey-Hawkins], are deficit-neutral--Pro-Market "win-win" solutions:

The American people win, and capitalism wins—

Jim Green, Democrat candidate for Congress, 2000

CHAPTER FIFTEEN

To Whom It May Concern—in Washingon:

OUR CHOICES ARE: Adapt and change in a world that is changing, whether we like it or not, OR be forced to create a Police State to hold our anachronistic policies, practices and laws in place—

And in America, today, we have chosen the latter…..and as only one pernicious example, of thousands—Ferguson is the result….

In a comedic, but religious context we hear of persons asking God for a sign—anything—which will warn us that we are on the wrong path, and need to change direction…..and our Police State choice, above, is *our sign*…..few are listening….

To illustrate a critical area in which we need to adapt and change in a 21st Century economy: We have far more work that needs to be done in America, than we have persons to fill these jobs—And 86% of Americans believe that "Anybody wanting to work should be able to find a job"---So, why on earth *in a democracy*, do we have 9 million jobless Americans—[per the 11/14 DOL Jobs report]?

The answer is because our *method* of job creation in America is based on a Fairy Tale! Specifically, our current *one and only* job creation methodology in America, is based on the myth/sacred cow:

"The market can provide anybody wanting a job, with a job"—

Problem is—it is pure BS—and only *once* since WW II has this methodology resulted in an unemployment rate below 3%--in 1953 [i.e., which translates into 5 million left jobless]--because the market *cannot* create enough jobs—in short, the jobs for this 5 million jobless--*don't exist*!

The right-wing propaganda mills trick our fools into believing that the market has created this 5 million jobs, but because those on welfare are "lazy and don't want to work" this 5 million jobs go unfilled—but that is *pure balderdash!*

The vast majority of persons on welfare, are there *because* the *market* cannot create enough jobs, i.e., the market lacks the viability to create these jobs—the jobs simply *do not exist*!

And as further proof, according to the CBO, on our current path it will be 2017 before America returns to even an anemic 5.5% unemployment rate [following the Great Recession] and if the market fails in the interim—the jobless are out of luck!

Further, this travesty is compounded because the Republicans cling to devious and discredited Supply Side Economics [to this day] as a solution, to wit:

Siphon America's wealth away from the consuming middle—give this windfall of cash to the Koch Bros [a metaphor for the 1%, hereafter "KB"]—they will build factories all across our fair land—everyone will have a job in the corporation—and we will all live happily ever after—Yes, folks it is a fairy tale!

And what we learned from this dark cloud over America is what Bush I called it long ago—before America was subjected to this devious scam—i.e., Supply-Side is "VooDoo Economics"!

So why have we allowed ourselves to be deceived by this Republican scam—[handcrafted by a plutocracy/oligarchy that still has one foot on the plantation]? But I don't want to giveaway the surprise ending—and some of my response isn't printable....! Further, and to say it up front....I am a capitalist—I support 100%: Build a better widget, sell it for a million bucks, and retire in South Florida....it is the Republican agenda, today, that is anti-market...more on this throughout.....

When President Carter handed the reigns over to Reagan in 1981—he left America with a very modest $60 billion deficit—as a direct result of Supply-Side, however, when Republicans held the White House [Clinton actually cut the deficit]—this $60 billion ballooned to a staggering $10 trillion by 2008—and it has cost Americans an additional $7+trillion to clean up this Republican mess—

Ask any economist: Our only way out of a meltdown *is to buy our way out!* [it was the lesson learned from the Great Depression].

And anyone who thinks McCain, had he been elected, would not have addressed this with a Stimulus, the same as President Obama in 2009—is stuffed between the ears with rice pudding……

Further, we learned that we cannot siphon America's wealth away from the consuming middle, and give it to the "KB"—without sending our economy into meltdown—as occurred in 1987 and 2008—in short, the Supply-Side scam has a shelf-life of about 7 years before the economy collapses—and as noted, costing the taxpayers trillions to put a floor under a disappearing economy!

And another fallout/direct result from this dark chapter is the disparity in wealth it has created in America—AKA the "wealth gap"--and currently the "richest 1 percent in the United States now own more wealth than the bottom 90 percent"—the second highest in our history, the first was just before the Great Depression.

A couple of other factors that played into the above scenario—when every waking moment in capitalism is spent pondering how to eliminate as many of us humans, as possible, from the workplace—to increase "profits"—why, on Earth, would we look to the market to solve our unemployment crisis in America?

As well, few things on earth are more unstable than the market….we can count on one hand the number of corporations in America that were around in 1900….with tens of thousands long since disappeared; and given "automation", alone, the market will produce fewer and fewer jobs the further we advance into the 21st Century.

Further, unemployment is a "social" problem—we, as the larger society have the responsibility to solve—i.e., it is unrealistic to expect the market to solve this problem—the market is in the "for profit" business, not the social work business—and the former would not long be in business--if they were…for example, we should never condemn the CEO for closing a plant when they are losing money—but we should be outraged by a government that doesn't have a clue re the displaced employees…..

Also, unemployment is a *no one wins* …..the jobless lose, and market loses, to wit:

> 3% is the zero-sum threshold above which unemployment triggers inflation by diminishing labor training and skills, under-utilizing capital resources, reducing the rate of productivity advance, increasing unit labor costs, and reducing the general supply of goods and services--and the loss in income to the Market is compounded exponentially with each percentage point of increase in unemployment, above 3%.

Short Definition:

3% is the zero-sum threshold above which unemployment starts substantially undermining the Market--and the loss in income to the Market is compounded exponentially with each percentage point of increase in unemployment, above 3%.

In sum, our job creation should be based on: Fix unemployment, and this will fix the market [HR 1000], rather than [our current mind-set] Fix the market, and this in turn fix unemployment [HR 2847] – with a result that has been a disaster—as we inch along in our job recovery, see data above, and when we didn't *Fix Unemployment* a retaliatory electorate ushered in a House filled with lunatics in the 2010 election, and then doubled down in 2014!

Look around—all signs in our economy are up—and yet over two-thirds of our rank and file believe "we are moving in the wrong direction"—their perception is that our economy is in the tank—that we are in an economic malaise—a condition that would disappear overnight if we did, in fact, *Fix Unemployment*!

Best guess is that Congress passed, and President Obama signed into law HR 2847 [the HIRE Act], in 2009—which is based on fix the market, and this will fix unemployment [180 degrees off course]—but they did this because of the pervasive [but false] *belief* that

"The market can provide anybody wanting a job, with a job"—it is *pure BS……it doesn't work*! Had we insisted on putting a lawnmower engine in the rocket to get us to the Moon….we would never have gotten there…[same difference]….and all of the empirical evidence is proof HR 2847 didn't create anywhere near the jobs needed…

Jim Green, Democrat opponent to Lamar Smith, Congress, 2000

CHAPTER SIXTEEN

HOPPER-READY: THE NEIGHBOR-TO-NEIGHBOR JOB CREATION ACT

[1] PROPOSED LEGISLATION:

THE NEIGHBOR-TO-NEIGHBOR JOB CREATION ACT

A Pro-Market, deficit-neutral, federally mandated, Social Insurance, owned by our employed, to provide a fund to hire/train our unemployed.

SECTION 1. SHORT TITLE.

> This Act shall be cited as The Neighbor-To-Neighbor Job Creation Act [To establish employment/training opportunities for the unemployed in compliance with the "Legal Authorization" in Public Law 15 USC § 3101, for the creation of a "reservoir of public employees", anytime our unemployment rate exceeds "3%", with an emphasis on training for market needs, including a training stipend, where there is a shortage of trained workers--hereafter NTN].

SEC. 2. DEFINITIONS.

In this Act the following definitions apply:
> (1) SECRETARY- The term `Secretary' means the Secretary of Labor.
> (2) STATE- The term `State' has the meaning given such term in section 102(2) of the Housing and Community Development Act (42 U.S.C. 5302(2)).
> (3) TRUST FUND- The term `Trust Fund' refers to the Department of Labor Full Employment Trust Fund.
> (4) UNIT OF GENERAL LOCAL GOVERNMENT- The term `unit of general local government' has the meaning given such term in section 102(1) of the Housing and Community Development Act (42 U.S.C. 5302(1)).
> (5) URBAN COUNTY- The term `urban county' has the meaning given such term in section 102(6) of the Housing and Community Development Act (42 U.S.C. 5302(6)).
> (6) WEB SITE- The Secretary shall establish an Internet Web site to serve as an information clearinghouse for job training and employment opportunities funded by the Trust Fund.

SEC. 3. EMPLOYMENT OPPORTUNITY GRANTS TO STATES, LOCAL GOVERNMENT.

(a) Use of Funds-A recipient of a grant under this section shall use the grant primarily for infrastructure repair, including, but not limited to:

(A) The painting and repair of schools, community centers, and libraries.
(B) The restoration and revitalization of abandoned and vacant properties to alleviate blight in distressed and foreclosure-affected areas of a unit of general local government.
(C) The augmentation of staffing in Head Start, child care, and other early childhood education programs to promote school readiness and early literacy.
(D) The renovation and enhancement of maintenance of parks, playgrounds, and other public spaces.

Respectfully Submitted,

Jim Green, Democrat candidate for Congress, Dist 21, TX, 2000

CHAPTER SEVENTEEN

WHAT WE NEED TO DO GOING FORWARD IN THE 21ST CENTURY:

Inexplicably "public employment" is seen the same as WPA—where millions are employed directly by the federal government—when that model is not only outmoded—it is insufficient to address our problems in the 21st century.

What we need today is an expanding and contracting public workforce—that expands during downturns in the market, and contracts as employees return to the private sector [Google: The Buffer Stock Employment Model]—triggered anytime our unemployment exceeds "3%" [as "authorized" under Humphrey-Hawkins]-- and least understood: This is an INDISPENSABLE component in the effective functioning of our 21st Century Market.

The market thrives when we have a robust, employed, consuming workforce—our manufacturers are sitting on $2 trillion in cash because they do not have consumers for their products—i.e., absent consumers, they lay off employees—[and the Republican solution, Reaganomics, has acted as an accelerate to this downward spiral—and which Romney promises to return us to if he is elected]!

In short, the above model is a "win-win" solution—the American people win, and capitalism wins!

To achieve this, what is being urged is "The Neighbor-To-Neighbor Job Creation Act": A federally mandated, mutual insurance—owned by our employed [from janitor to CEO] to create a fund to hire/train our unemployed.

To be viable, however, our job creation solution <u>*MUST*</u> contain:

1] Be based on the premise that we have far more work that needs to be done in America, than we have persons to fill these jobs.

2] It MUST have renewable funding.

3] It will not add a dime to our deficit.

To expand briefly, it is currently believed, erroneously, that we need "make work" jobs so that everyone who wants to work will have a job—but this is absurd—and an insult to "Yankee Ingenuity".

We do not have an unemployment crisis from a shortage of jobs, or money—but rather from a shortage of imagination.

Regarding "renewable funding" ALL of our job creation solutions, to date, have been based on the mind-set: "jump start" the market, and the market will in turn create all the jobs we need—and even setting aside that this is untrue, our current job creation is moving at a snail's pace—long past the unemployment benefits drying up—with the CBO projecting that even with the JOBS Act, signed into law on April 6, 2012--it will be 2017 before we return to a barely acceptable 5.5% unemployment rate!

Further, by its nature when we "jump start" --the employment ends when the funding runs out as we learned from the Stimulus—whereas any real fix to our unemployment crisis <u>*demands*</u> renewable funding….

And whether the electorate will accept an unemployment rate hovering around 8% on election day—is the $64,000 question….

Regarding not adding a dime to our deficit—under The Neighbor-To-Neighbor Job Creation Act [NTN], the <u>*funding*</u> to reduce our unemployment to 3% comes from an insurance owned by our employed, rather than added to our deficit—

If one is employed in America, participation in this insurance plan is mandatory—similar in concept to our auto insurance or Social Security Insurance [and without question the most successful social program in American history].

Jobs beget jobs--And with a modest policy cost of 4% of salary we can create more "private-sector" jobs in 6 months, that HR 2847, and the JOBS Act, in 6 years—and unlike these laws—NTN will not add a dime to our deficit!

Finally, this is in total concert with the will of the American people, i.e., that "anybody willing to work should be able to find a job"—and the American people have told our politicians time and again of their willingness to chip in to help their neighbor get a job [and as an _insurance_, as above, it also protects their continued employment]—it is just that Washington is deaf as an adder!

CHAPTER EIGHTEEN

President Obama/Council of Economic Advisers:

Public-Sector jobs strengthen our free-enterprise market economy—i.e., they are a critical component to the viability of our 21st Century economy--rather than weakening the market--as propagandist, with one foot on the plantation, fraudulently deceive the public into believing for the purposes of exploiting American employees…..

Indeed, since WW II, the Koch brothers [both literally, and a metaphor, here, for the 1%] have spent tens of millions buying governors and legislators, to cement "at will" employment in every state [and currently only Montana limits to probationary employees]; and to destroy "collective bargaining", i.e., unions in America—

In sum, they have spent tens of millions of dollars to destroy "employee rights" in America!

To understand the importance of "collective bargaining" for employees, it is informative to take a page from history:

When Hitler became the dictator in Germany, one of his first laws was to make it illegal for more than three persons to gather on the street—and German citizens were subject to immediate arrest if they did.

The same principal is being used by preventing employees putting their heads together, as it were, to bargain for employee rights—and recently one group of employees placed "job security" over a salary increase—with the irony being that the specific objective of "at will" employment—is to destroy "job security"!

In short, the deceptive propaganda to frighten Americans regarding "public-sector" jobs, has but a single parent: To exploit American labor—by some, to assuage deep-seated feelings of inferiority [they can only feel tall, by making others small, in their eyes]-–– but most often for just pure GREED!

Where our policies makers go wrong by pandering to some in the oligarchy—and/or buying into this fraudulent propaganda:

Unemployment is a NO ONE WINS—the jobless lose, civility loses, and the market loses, to wit:

THE LAW OF DIMINISHED INCOME TO THE MARKET FROM UNEMPLOYMENT [hereafter D/UE LAW]

Short Definition:

> 3% is the zero-sum threshold above which unemployment starts substantially undermining the Market--and the loss in income tthe Market is compounded exponentially with each percentage point of increase in unemployment, above 3%.

Ref: IT IS IMPOSSIBLE TO BE A CHRISTIAN, AND
VOTE REPUBLICAN, Amazon

Jim Green, Democrat opponent to Lamar Smith, 2000

CHAPTER NINETEEN

I didn't write the following. It is a cut and paste from FACEBOOK, or some blog [would like to give credit if knew the author]--but it is so on target regarding how "fear" is driving Conservative policy in America today—i.e., is undermining America and our progress—and relegating America to a Third World country status, rather than a world leader—FDR had it on the nose in "All we have to fear, is fear itself"…at his inaugural in 1933….

"Conservatives are such cowards: they are afraid of gay people getting married or serving in the military; they are afraid of bringing terrorists to super max prisons in the US from which no one has ever escaped; they are afraid of the boy scouts letting gay kids in; they are afraid of everyone voting and are constantly suppressing the vote under some bogus voter fraud theory; they are afraid of letting students vote at their universities; they are afraid of women having the right to choose; they even are afraid of women getting contraception [the real issue actually is a women's agency and control over their bodies]; they are afraid of immigration reform leading to citizenship because they are afraid of-- name whatever reason; they are afraid of mandating gun purchasers to undergo background checks for crazy people and terrorists; they are afraid of people smoking pot; they are afraid of climate change being real and contradicting their beloved Bible; they are afraid of legitimate campaign reform; they are afraid of Muslims; they are afraid of blacks; they are afraid of atheists; they are afraid of hippies; they are afraid of socialists; they are probably still afraid of monsters under their beds; they are just rank cowards and keep making things up to be afraid of."

CHAPTER TWENTY

[I couldn't resist including this…and yes I am the author…..]

A MESSAGE FROM GOD

MANY CENTURIES AGO, a man of the cloth, we don't know his name, and in a flash of insight (perhaps induced by peyote) told his flock that "sex is a sin". And lo and behold he learned that by taking a very natural and healthy part of our life and turning it into something that was "dirty and nasty", that he could imprison his flock, and fill his coffers, and hallelujah it was a great day for the Lord!

Quickly, his miracle spread to other churches in his village, and then to the next village, and then the next county, and then state, and soon it spread to all the churches in the ancient world, and all of their flocks cowed in fear and shame and became imprisoned, and their coffers over-floweth. Hallelujah, it was a great day for the Lord!

And to keep the myth alive they started inventing stories, half-baked stories, that made no sense to anyone who is rational, such as "Mary was a virgin"—well, she just had to be a virgin because she would never partake in anything that was dirty and nasty, like sex (if you're doing it right), and this was necessary to make "sex is a sin" make sense…so they invented a Mary that was "sinless"--you get the picture. And their coffers over-floweth. Hallelujah, it was a great day for the Lord!

No one seemed to be bothered that when we play tricks on the human mind by taking something that is very natural and healthy, such as sex, and make it dirty and nasty that all kinds of bad things happen to the human mind:

Such as most pedophiles, and most serial killers, and voting Republican, and unwarranted suicides, and most mental illness, and unwanted pregnancies. (Teens not wanting to have sex is the perversion, not the other way around, and by replacing sex education and condoms, with unrealistic "abstinence", and by using blather about "low self-esteem" to shame them into not "sinning"—We have a teen pregnancy in the U.S. twice that of England and Canada!).

But none of this mattered, because their coffers over-floweth, and Hallelujah, it is a great day for the Lord!

There is a cure--------Tell our right-wing hypocrites, who Judge, rather than "Judge not".... to shove it....

GOD

ABOUT THE AUTHOR: I was employed in our Criminal Justice System for a cumulative 20 years as a probation officer, with 5 of those years as a chief probation officer. I authored the concept of "Shock Incarceration" which became law in Kansas in 1970, and then was adopted in numerous jurisdictions in the U.S. and also spread to Europe—it is currently identified in the U.S. as "Boot Camp" [as the means to "shock" the young offender—and a total distortion of my original intent—like many ideas, once released, they take on a life of their own]. I also instigated establishment of the first Court Psychiatric Clinic in the U.S., in conjunction with psychiatrists from the Menninger Foundation, as a chief probation officer. Finally, I was the Democrat candidate for Congress, District 21, TX, 2000. I would most define myself as a Social Ecologist-- [albeit my degree is in Psychology]. My web page is www.Inclusivism.org –which has been on the internet since 1996.
http://www.amazon.com/James-L.-Jim-Green/e/B001KHZIMM/ref=ntt_dp_epwbk_0

A BRIEF ADDENDUM: When the U.S. Supreme Court denied certiorari—where a federal judge falsified a federal court record with the SPECIFIC intent to deny my protected rights under the U.S.Constitution [TO DENY TO ME RIGHTS OF U.S. CITIZENSHIP!]….and to cover up criminal negligence on the part of the government defendants in the death of our son—[detailed in THE HARVARD BOYS CLUB, Amazon/Kindle]--I filed a Petition for Rehearing [which is automatic]—and included the following. The Clerk of the U.S. Supreme Court called me at my office in California, and asked that I withdraw the "cartoon" [a reprint from The NEW YORKER] from my Petition. I refused on the basis of the First Amendment, and it remains in the archives at the U.S. Supreme Court [Docket #: 79-1627], to this day. The wording [not that clear] is: "Excellent, excellent. A fine blend of truths, half-truths, and blatant falsehoods".

IN THE
Supreme Court of the United States
October Term, 1979
No. 79-1627

JAMES L. GREEN,
Petitioner,
vs.

"Excellent, excellent. A fine blend of truths, half-truths, and blatant falsehoods."

OTHER BOOKS BY THIS AUTHOR ON AMAZON/KINDLE/BN:

- **THE HARVARD BOYS CLUB:** Hitler's Assault On Our Freedoms From His Grave
- **MY LETTERS TO PRESIDENT OBAMA:** Confessions Of A Compulsive Letter Writer
- **OUR GREED AND IGNORANCE:** Poses A Far Greater Threat To America, Than Terrorism
- **LETTERS ON STEROIDS:** Confessions Of A Compulsive Letter-To-The-Editor Writer
- **THE FIRST TIME I HAD SEX:** And, The Religious Intolerance Attack On America
- **WHY PRESIDENT OBAMA LOST THE 2012 ELECTION:** A Wake-Up Call
- **ECONOMIC INCLUSIVISM:** Neo-Capitalism/An Anthology: Inclusive pro-market solutions to our social problems
- **AMERICA IS ONE SICK MF:** Why Greed-Driven America Went Off The Rails….
- **EVERY GIVEN SUNDAY:** A Scientific Formula To Predict NFL Games

And others….http://www.amazon.com/James-L.-Jim-Green/e/B001KHZIMM/ref=ntt_dp_epwbk_0

www.ingramcontent.com/pod-product-compliance
Lightning Source LLC
Chambersburg PA
CBHW030452220526
45464CB00006B/2503